Always Room for Christmas Pud

Aunty Donna

ANNIVERSARY
30
YEARS
EDITION

Illustrated by
James Fosdike

'When you invest in pud, you invest in your friends.'

Mark Samual Bonanno

About the Author

Aunty Donna is a prominent Australian children's book author. She is a famous recluse with the only image available being this Archibald Prize–winning self-portrait. In the 1990s and early 2000s her work redefined the Australian children's book canon with many now-grown-ups in the fields of literature, film, music and comedy citing her as a foundational influence.

More recently, Aunty Donna has developed a keen interest in exploring the limits of both national and international copyright law, which has seen her make headlines all around the globe. She still self-publishes children's books that explore a narrow range of topics close to her heart.

Also by Aunty Donna

Published for Children

Timmy and the Fly-Blown Ewe (1990)

Always Room for Christmas Pud (1992)

The Good, the Bad and the Cowdoy (1995)

The Brown Snake and the Three-Hour Drive to Hospital (1996)

(Walking in on Someone) Doing a Poo (2000)

Salvatore Michaelangelo and His Disgruntled Adventure to the IGA (2002)

The Necromantic Pudding (2005)

Published for Adults

Desire and the Byzantine Empire (330–1453 CE) (2004)

Self-Published for Children

Mr Penguin Is Actually a Penguin (2007)

How Penguins Lie and Dress Like People (2008)

The Young Wizard Boy and His Magical High School (2011)
(under investigation for plagiarism)

The Nosy Journalist and the Two Broken Thumbs (2012)

They Track You Through Your Phone (2014)

The Rather Quite Peckish Centipede (2015)
(under investigation for plagiarism)

The Courts Are Broken (2016)

oBikes and Your Data (2018)

Where's Warren? (2020)
(under investigation for plagiarism)

That Penguin Won't Get Away With This (2022)

Foreword

Mark, Zach and Broden

Aunty Donna *(Sketch Comedy Group)*

It was just like any other regular day at primary school. It was the dying days of Term Four, and as lunchtime was drawing to a close and the harsh Australian sun was burning the necks of children who had forgotten their legionnaire hats, Broden was dominating the Grade Ones at four square, Mark was faking a sick tum in the sick bay, and Zach was doing a big poo.

But that afternoon, something amazing happened. Our Grade Three teacher, Mrs Upton, read a storybook to the class. It was an honest tale. A simple tale. And it was unlike anything we had ever heard. It is no exaggeration when we say that there is not a single other work in existence that has inspired us more than Aunty Donna's 1992 classic *Always Room for Christmas Pud*. This book wasn't about supernatural marsupials or famished insects – and, unlike other fictional puddings out there, the pudding at the story's centre wasn't magic, self-replenishing or belligerent. It was simply rich and delicious. The way in which Aunty Donna captured that intersection of dense dessert and human frailty struck something deep within us, and we knew we were going to spend the rest of our lives attempting to create works as powerful as this.

We like to joke (or lie) about the origins of our sketch comedy gang, but this seems like a fitting time to finally tell the truth. Not many people know that we did, in fact, meet at primary school. Many have guessed that the name of our humble little comedy troupe was inspired by this very author. Some have even guessed that we have based our signature looks on the characters from this book. A few go so far as to say that perhaps some of our more popular sketches draw light inspiration from stories originally written by the great Aunty Donna herself. To those people we say: 'No comment.'

Although we have never met Aunty Donna in real life, we have exchanged many an email with her copyright lawyers, and as her case against us is still working its way through the judicial system we are unable to comment on such conversations at this point in time. We do, however, hope that one day she will emerge from her shell so that we may simply say to her, 'Thank you. Thank you, for everything' and 'Please stop suing us.'

Anyway, considering all that, it really is quite baffling we were asked to write a foreword to this new edition. But whatever, it's fine.

A message from Mr Penguin

Before we begin, I want to get ahead of the rumours and address that I am in fact a human man, and not a penguin. The only thing about me that has anything to do with penguins is my name and, by extension, the name of my company. I trust I will not need to mention this again.

For thirty years, *Always Room for Christmas Pud* has delighted and thrilled audiences of all ages. From the moment I started my company thirty-four years ago, I knew that I wanted to publish only the best books under my eponymous brand. That is why I, Mr Penguin, am proud to bring you this thirtieth-anniversary hardback or paperback edition, depending on what edition you bought, as we'll probably publish both a hardback and a paperback edition, but I've only had time to write one introduction, so hopefully I've covered both bases here. Despite both my company and me personally having now severed all ties with Aunty Donna, this publication marked a watershed moment in Australian children's publishing – an achievement to be celebrated and revered.

I know I said I wouldn't mention this again, but to be clear, Aunty Donna and I parted ways after she publicly accused me of being an actual penguin and not a human man. It is a great shame that Aunty Donna chose to smear my name with such a vicious rumour, but, as the media rightly publicised, it was a rumour without evidence or any foundation in truth.

I have fond memories of working with Aunty Donna on all of her books, but I've always had a particular soft spot for *Always Room for Christmas Pud.* It is a stupendous story of mateship, festivity and, of course, pud. Having been translated into more than thirty-three languages, this uniquely Australian story transcends age, nationality and culture. And, despite the ridiculous allegations Aunty Donna has levelled against me, I still take a great deal of pride in what we created together.

I mean, a penguin?! Think about it. How could I even be a penguin? That doesn't make any sense. What, are you suggesting that a little penguin somehow waddled their way up from Antarctica, learned to speak human, and then convinced everyone they were a human man? That's so stupid. I mean, even if they could do that, do you think anyone would let them run and operate a successful publishing company?! Or decide which Penguin Classics titles will be printed onto mugs?! Shut up.

Seriously, look at the picture. That's me. Now, you tell me – is that a man or is that a little penguin dressed in a tuxedo sporting a top hat and cane? Clearly that's a man. Human men wear top hats and, like, when have you ever seen a penguin wear a top hat? Doesn't happen. And I am legit wearing a top hat in that pic so . . . what else do I even need to say? Case closed, if you ask me.

Please enjoy this special anniversary edition of *Always Room for Christmas Pud*.

Mr Penguin

Christmas dinner was done,
'twas one of the greats!

Where once was a banquet
just lay empty plates.

The prawns and bean salad
and ham were so yummy,

Now all that remained were
the guests with full tummies.

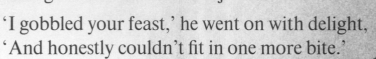

'That dinner was perfect, from entree to roast!'
One guest exclaimed to his jubilant host.

'I gobbled your feast,' he went on with delight,
'And honestly couldn't fit in one more bite.'

'But, ho!' said the host. 'How I wish that you could,
For in my possession I have CHRISTMAS PUD.'

'Awww, maybe a little,'
the guest did reply,

With a grin on his face
and a glint in his eye.

'Thanks, but no thanks,' cried the third at the table.
'I've no room for pud and thus I'm unable.'

So, the host didn't push it,
though proud of his pud,

For he knew that his offer
was just far too good.

Soon enough, to be sure,
Diner Three did agree.

'Oh, maybe a little.
A small pud for me.'

For as much as they'd eaten all that they could . . .

There's always room for Christmas pud.

And oh, what a pud that he'd made for them all.
So nutty and fruity! This tasty moist ball.

With a knife in his hand,
the host then enquired

How large of a portion
that each guest desired.

'There's room in my tum,'
Diner Three did admit,

'But just for a tiny,
most minimal bit.'

'And make mine so petite
that it's barely a sliver!'

'Like this . . . ?'

'Oh, maybe a little bit bigger.'

The guests eyed their bowls, full of pud to the brim.
They wondered aloud how they'd squeeze it all in!

But the pud was not all that our good host had mustered.

'Oh . . . you didn't say there was custard.'

Ah, that sweet eggy sauce that does live in our dreams!
It is simply divine but best paired with fresh cream.

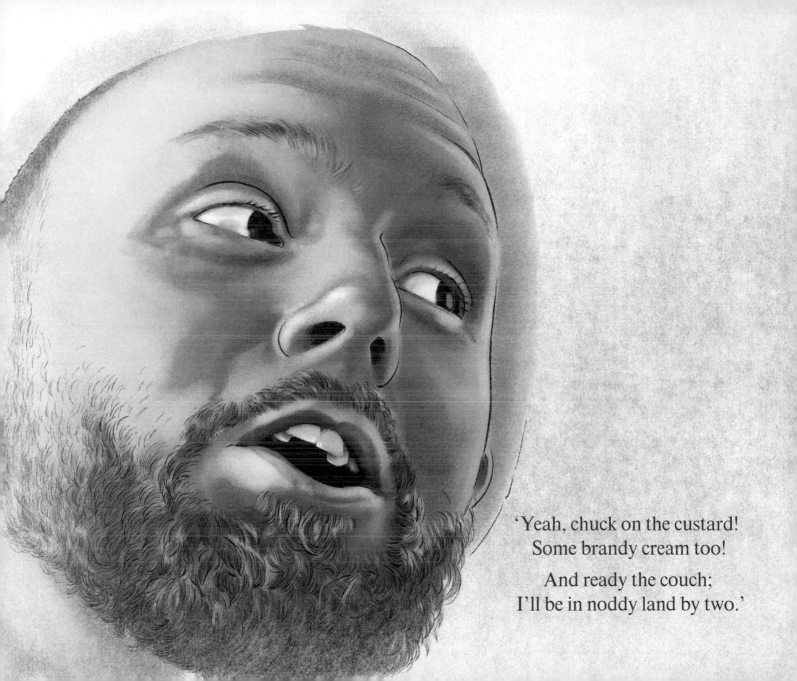

'Yeah, chuck on the custard!
Some brandy cream too!

And ready the couch;
I'll be in noddy land by two.'

'I'm a big ol' boofhead,'
cried the host to his guests,

For he'd made too much pud –
more than they could digest.

But the guests disagreed,
and one stopped the host's yappin'.

'What's the rush?' he cried out.

'Leave it there. See what happens.'

Well, can you believe? They had two serves of pud!
Two serves is two more than they said that they would!

Oh, double the pud – it's quite simply absurd.

But the host, he was thinking of offering a third . . .

Now, 'third time's
the charm' is a motto
that's said.

But three times the pud?
That should fill one
with dread!

For yes, while it's tasty
and yummy and good,

There is such a thing as . . .

TOO MUCH PUD.

Book club notes

When presented with a Christmas pud after a large dinner, two guests must question their long-held and seemingly reasonable beliefs that they are too full and couldn't fit in another bite.

Always Room for Christmas Pud is a classic tale that interrogates the thin moral line between a full tummy and a tummy with enough room for pud, making it a perfect book to discuss with your book club – no matter the time of year.

- Were you familiar with the concept of there being extra room in one's stomach for pud? If so, did this book change your opinion of that concept? If not, what discoveries did you make while reading the book?

- At one point in the book, one of the guests says to the host 'Oh, you didn't say there was custard'. Do you think this was a genuine reaction? If not, what do you think their underlying motive might have been?

- The host laments that he made too much pud. Do you think this is true? Do you think his choice to make too much pud was, in fact, deliberate? Why?

- The guests ultimately fail in their quest to tread the line between the right amount of pud and too much pud. What do you think the author is trying to convey with this narrative choice?

- One of the guests has long hair and one of the guests has no hair at all. Discuss.

Acknowledgements

Aunty Donna (Sketch Comedy Group)
Jo Ruane
Katherine Dale and the team at Century Entertainment
James Fosdike and the team at Jacky Winter
Isabelle Yates, Adam Laszczuk and the team at Penguin Random House
Our families
Our partners (aka kissing friends!!!)

Aunty Donna (Author)
I do not approve of this new edition and I will not be sending
acknowledgements to none of you dogs. Don't contact me again.

Mr Penguin
The Antarctic and Southern Ocean Coalition
Guiseppa's No Questions Asked Tailoring
Altona Fish Wholesalers
Luc Jacquet

James Fosdike
Amy (wife), George (son), Goose (dog) and Aunty Donna (boys).
But not my cat. Total boofhead.

PENGUIN BOOKS

UK | USA | Canada | Ireland | Australia
India | New Zealand | South Africa | China

Penguin Books is part of the Penguin Random House group of companies
whose addresses can be found at global.penguinrandomhouse.com

Penguin
Random House
Australia

First published by Penguin Books in 2022

Cover and internal illustrations by James Fosdike
Cover design by Adam Laszczuk © Penguin Random House Australia Pty Ltd
Internal design by Adam Laszczuk

Printed and bound in China by RR Donnelley Asia Printing Solutions Ltd

A catalogue record for this
book is available from the
National Library of Australia

ISBN 978 0 14377 981 0

penguin.com.au

We at Penguin Random House Australia acknowledge that Aboriginal and Torres Strait Islander peoples
are the Traditional Custodians and the first storytellers of the lands on which we live and work.
We honour Aboriginal and Torres Strait Islander peoples' continuous connection to Country,
waters, skies and communities. We celebrate Aboriginal and Torres Strait Islander stories,
traditions and living cultures; and we pay our respects to Elders past and present.

Aunty Donna* are an absurdist comedy collective from Melbourne formed of
Mark Samual Bonanno, Broden Kelly, Zachary Ruane, Sam Lingham, Max Miller and
Tom Armstrong. In 2020 they released their Netflix series, *Aunty Donna's Big Ol' House of Fun*,
to rave reviews. Aunty Donna's energetic live shows have seen them sell out theatres
all around the world and they've created hit web series such as *1999* and
Glennridge Secondary College. In 2018 they released and toured an album called
The Album and they recently recorded the 300th episode of *The Aunty Donna Podcast*.

The inspiration for a sketch of cult status that's been watched online over
five million times, *Always Room for Christmas Pud* is their first book.**

*Not to be confused with the children's author of the same name, who is real and wrote this book.
**That they have written an introduction for.

James Fosdike was discovered by Wil Anderson on a dark and stormy night,
in a basket at his front door. Never one to turn away those less fortunate,
Wil took James under his wing (he's secretly a bird) and enrolled James in
the Sir Douglas Mawson Institute of TAFE, specifically a Certificate IV
course in Advertising and Graphic Design. Unfortunately James became lost in
the off-campus TAFE lifestyle and failed to complete the course.